ABOUT THE BOOK

While other children were playing "follow the leader" along the great stone wall near Lyme Regis, Mary Ann Anning would be climbing the nearby cliffs with her father in search of curiosities. Many people believed that the strange shells they found were children of stones, or thunderbolts dropped from the sky.

One morning as Mary approached the cliffs something unusual caught her eye. As she chipped along the soft rock, an enormous skeleton began to appear. What could it be? People came running from miles around to see the monstrous curiosity. Some thought it was a dragon. For years it was known as "The Mystery of Lyme Regis."

As Ruth Van Ness Blair tells the true story of Mary Ann Anning's momentous discovery of the Ichthyosaurus, a fascinating picture of a world where people were just beginning to think in a scientific way unfolds. Engaging, colorful descriptions of English life in the 1800's and of the excitement generated by Mary's fantastic find are detailed in lively well-researched illustration by Richard Cuffari.

MARY'S MONSTER

by RUTH VAN NESS BLAIR
illustrated by Richard Cuffari

Coward, McCann & Geoghegan, Inc.
New York

published simultaneously in Canada by
Longman Canada Limited, Toronto.

SBN:GB-698-30556-6
SBN:TR-698-20304-6

Library of Congress Catalog Card Number: 74-16651

PRINTED IN THE UNITED STATES OF AMERICA

designed by Cathy Altholz

CONTENTS

Mary's World

Many years ago—long before automobiles, airplanes, radio, and television were invented—a little girl was born in the town of Lyme Regis on the southern coast of England. Her name was Mary Ann Anning.

Mary's birthplace was first heard of in 774 when the land at the mouth of the Lym river was used for "salt boiling"—a way of getting salt from the waters of Lyme Bay. More than a thousand years later, Lyme Regis had become a busy and pleasant little town in a busy and sometimes unpleasant world.

Mary was born in a time when men were tired of conflict. The troublesome Revolutionary war with the American colonies was barely over when the bloody French Revolution began. This war, and the unrest which followed it, worried the British. All they wanted now, was to continue trade with France and to be able to visit there without fear.

England was rich. But because of rising food prices, many poor people did not have enough to eat.

New machines for spinning and weaving were invented and put to use in great factories. Country people moved to the cities to work. This caused overcrowding and slums.

The factories and homes burned coal because wood was scarce.

The smoke from thousands of these fires and the dense English fog formed heavy smog over the large cities.

In London, a hundred and fifty miles from Lyme Regis, there was crime in the streets. It was an anxious world. In fact, Mary's world was a little like ours.

People were beginning to pull away from ignorance and superstition. They began to think in a scientific way about the wonders of their earth.

Those who could read had a choice of many good books. Two of them were Defoe's "Robinson Crusoe," and Fielding's "Tom Jones." But the favorites of many of the readers were the horror stories. They had frightening names such as "The Demon of Sicily," "The Mysterious Hand," and "The Mysteries of Udolpho." Most of these books were written by women.

George the Third was king of England. But he was having a bad time of it. He had lost his American colonies. They were now the United States of America, governed by a president.

Mary was born May 21, 1799. In that same year, George Washington, the first president of the United States, died, and Napoleon Bonaparte became the First Consul of France.

This was the world of Mary Ann Anning.

CHAPTER ONE

"One, Two, Buckle My Shoe"

Mary's morning chores were almost finished. The beds were made, the breakfast porridge bowls and tea mugs washed and put away. Mary had one task left. She picked up a broom and opened the front door.

She stood for a moment on the stoop of the thatched stone cottage in which she lived, and looked about her.

Mary lived on Bridge Street near the little river, Lym. From her front door she could see the main street of town. Like Mary's street, it was lined with shops and cottages. It ran north and south. The north end climbed upwards toward a turf-covered cliff. At its very edge perched a church which gave the cliff its name —Church Cliff.

From there, the street hurried south to Lyme Bay. Beyond the town and the sparkling waters of the bay stood the great stone wall called the Cobb. It curved about the west end of the beach and jutted out into the water, forming a quiet harbor. Its sturdy walls served both as a break-water and a pier. The southwest winds which made Lyme Regis so pleasant in the summer could roar into great gales in the winter. The Cobb was strongly built in order to hold back the high tides which these winds hurled against the beach. It had been there for a long time—since the reign of Edward the First in the thirteenth century.

As Mary began to sweep the front steps, her father, Richard Anning, came to the door.

"It's a fair morning, daughter," he said. "A good time to go curiosity hunting."

Mary dropped the broom. "May we go, father? May we?" More than anything else she loved to hunt for the curious stone shells she and her father found in the cliffs and on the beach near Lyme Regis. It was a hobby they had enjoyed together since Mary was a small girl.

Mr. Anning smiled. "Later, daughter," he said. "When I have finished my work. It seems that on a fine day everyone in Lyme Regis has need of a carpenter." He glanced up and down

the street. "What a pity so many of us must stay inside on such a pleasant Saturday morning."

The shopkeepers had been at work for hours. Mary's mother, and many of the other women of Lyme Regis were now busy at their spinning wheels and looms. They had less than three months to make yards and yards of cloth and lace, and dozens of stockings to sell at the trade fair which was held in Lyme Regis every February first.

The November air was spring-like, and so still that the voices of the cement makers and the quarrymen could be heard from the gravel pits and quarries near town.

Mr. Anning turned to go back into the cottage. "The sooner I get to work, the sooner I finish," he said.

As he spoke, the sound of wheels and horses' hooves was heard at the top of the cliffs behind the town.

"It's the stagecoach," cried Mary. She put aside her broom and ran into the street.

The road that led down into Lyme Regis was steep and rough. The coachman did not seem to notice. With a crack of the whip he urged the four lathered horses down the hill and on to the main street at a break-neck speed.

The dusty stagecoach rocked from side to side. Suddenly one of the horses tripped on a rock. As he fell, he pulled the other horses down, and the stagecoach tipped over.

The valises, hat boxes, mail bags, and baskets on top of the stagecoach flew in every direction. Two gentlemen sitting on the high seats jumped off as the coach capsized. The ladies inside screamed. The poor coachman landed in a patch of prickly thistles! What a to-do!

The children of Lyme Regis dropped their hoops and their skipping ropes, and rushed to the overturned carriage. Mary, and her brother, Joseph, followed them.

Every door along the street opened.

Adults poured out of the buildings and joined the children.

Mr. Henley, the lord of the nearby manor, ran to the coachman.

"Why such haste, man," he shouted as he helped him up. "Need you drive so fast?"

Several quarrymen, the wheelwright, and Mr. Anning hurried to the aid of the passengers. They helped the horses right themselves. No one was hurt. The horses were only frightened.

The two ladies in the coach were quite annoyed. Their long, full skirts were covered with dust, and their bonnets knocked awry.

"What *is* this world coming to," they cried. "Why must everyone in England be in such a hurry?"

The coachman dusted off his trousers and mumbled, "That wretched road! How was I to know rocks had fallen across it?"

"It stormed yesterday," said Mr. Henley. "At this time of year the rain and wind cause rock and mud slides. Remember that, next time, and take it a bit slower into town. We can wait a few more minutes for our mail."

The coachman limped off grumpily to the inn. The passengers followed him. They were anxious to wash and rest. The townspeople slowly returned to their tasks. Stable boys led the horses and coach into the inn yard.

Now that the excitement was over, the children were no longer interested in the stagecoach.

"Come on," they yelled.

They raced down to the beach and began a wild game of "follow-the-leader" up and down the Cobb.

Mary and her brother did not join them. Joseph, who was three years older than his sister, returned to his job at the upholstery shop, and Mary ran back to the Anning cottage. She stopped at the door of her father's shop. He was hard at work.

Mrs. Anning saw her standing there.

"Mary Ann, do not bother your father," she said. "Go out and play while you have a chance."

"Yes, mother," Mary replied. She slowly left the house with her skipping rope in her hand.

The children on the beach had already tired of "follow-the-leader" and were now playing a noisy game of "French and English." Mary liked this game. It was a tug-of-war in which the loser was *always* the French.

She started down to the beach, but halfway there, she changed her mind. Suppose her father should finish his work quickly, and she wasn't home. It was better to stay near the cottage.

Mary picked up her skipping rope and started to skip. "One, two, buckle my shoe . . ." she began to chant.

In just a few minutes, Mr. Anning came to the door. "I've decided it's too fine a day to stay inside," he said. "I can finish my work tomorrow. Get your basket and hammer, lass. Let's go!"

So away went the two of them—to hunt for curiosities.

CHAPTER TWO

The Fossil Hunters

The best place to find curiosities was in the cliffs near Lyme Regis and at nearby Charmouth.

These cliffs were once part of the sea bottom. Millions of years ago, the ancestors of mollusks—soft creatures without backbones—died and drifted down to the ocean floor. Many of the mollusks were very like the snails and clams of today. These had outer shells. Others, with inner shells, resembled squid.

After a long time, the mollusks were covered with mud that slowly hardened. In most cases, the material of their shells was gradually replaced with minerals which became petrified—turned to stone.

Years later, when the sea bottom rose, it broke apart in places and cliffs were formed. In the rock of these cliffs could be seen the petrified shells and sometimes the original shells of the mollusks which had lived and died so long ago. These shells were the "curiosities" the Annings collected. Scientists called them "fossils."

Mary and her father soon discovered that yesterday's storm had broken great chunks of earth from the cliffs, exposing the rock underneath. They began their search in this rock and in the mud at the cliffs' base.

Almost at once, Mary found a curiosity which pleased her. She began to tap at it.

"Be patient, lass," her father said. "Use your hammer and chisel with great care. Curiosities are easily broken."

As the Annings worked their way along the cliffs, Mary asked, "What are curiosities, father? Where did they come from?"

"Some people say they are God's mistakes. Others say they were put there by the devil."

"Do you believe that, father?"

"No more than I believe they are decorations inside the earth, or that they are children of stones."

Mary sighed. "Does anyone *really* know?" she asked.

"Many years ago there was an artist named Leonardo da Vinci, who thought curiosities might be the remains of living creatures."

"Was he right, father?"

"I do not know, lass. But it does seem it might be true."

The sky which had been so bright and blue began to cloud up. The wind rose.

"What has happened to our beautiful day?" asked Mr. Anning.

Mary was not concerned with the change in the weather. She had just found a perfect curiosity in the mud at the base of the cliff. She held it out to her father.

"If this were a living creature, it must have died a long time ago."

Mr. Anning turned the shell over and over in his hand.

"I have heard tell of a Scotsman by the name of James Hutton," he said. "He believed there were worlds before our world. This curiosity you found may be what is left of a creature who lived in one of those other worlds."

Mary took the shell from her father and laid it gently in her basket.

"How long ago was the first world?"

"This man, Hutton, thought it was a long time ago."

"A thousand years?"

"Much more than that. Even Bishop Ussher of Ireland, who believed the world was always just as it is now, thought it was created 4,004 years before Christ."

"Was he right?"

"Some think not, lass. There are those who believe the world is much older and has changed many times. But who can tell!"

Thunder rumbled in the distance. Mr. Anning looked up at the clouded sky. "A storm is brewing. We'd best start for home."

Mary and her father set out at a fast pace. They scrambled up a steep path to the top of the cliffs, and raced across the grassy meadow. But the storm was ahead of them. Lightning flashed! The wind roared! Rain spilled from the sky, and the furious bay waters surged over the beach.

The lightning and swift rain frightened Mary. She ran for the shelter of a tree.

"No, lass, no," shouted her father. "Do not stand under the tree. Run for home!"

Mrs. Anning was waiting for them at the door when they arrived at the cottage.

"Richard," she cried, "You are soaking wet—and you with a bad cough! Mary Ann, *look* at you. Mud up to your knees!"

"Molly, Molly, you fret too much," said Mr. Anning. "I'm stronger than I look. And a little mud never hurt anyone."

After they had changed their clothes and were sipping hot tea, Mary said, "Father, why didn't you let me stand under the tree during the storm?"

"I will tell you a story," Richard Anning replied. "A true story.

"Once there was a little girl. She was put in care of a nurse. This nurse took the child to see a traveling horse show. While they were watching it, a violent storm came up.

"The nurse and two young women ran with the child to the shelter of a large elm tree. Lightning struck the tree and killed the three women. The child was knocked unconscious."

"Did she die?"

"No, daughter, she was revived. The doctor said it was a miracle."

"Who was she, father?"

Mr. Anning smiled. "You were the child, lass. I shall never forget the day. It was August 19, in the year 1800."

"I'm glad I'm still alive," Mary said.

"So am I," said her mother. "I need some one to help clear the table!"

As soon as the tea things were put away, Mary and her father emptied their baskets.

Most of the curiosities were curled shells called "horns of ammon." They were named after the Egyptian god, Ammon. His head was that of a ram with curled horns.

The cigar-shaped shells on the table were known as thunderstones. Many ignorant people believed they were petrified thunderbolts dropped from the sky during a thunderstorm. Mary and her father thought they might be the remains of sea creatures.

Mixed in with the horns of ammon and the thunderstones were heart shaped sea urchins, round sand dollars, and crooked clam shells called "devil's toenails."

Mary smiled at her father. "Today was a good hunting day,"

"Ah, yes," he replied. "The summer visitors will like these!"

CHAPTER THREE

The Summer Visitors

Every spring the people of Lyme Regis looked forward to the arrival of the stagecoaches filled with summer visitors.

Mr. Anning and Mary were especially glad to see them come. For now they could sell the curiosities they had collected all year. A carpenter did not earn very much, and any extra money was welcome.

Mary sat on the cottage steps and waited for the stagecoach. Today was her birthday. The air smelled of spring flowers and the sea. Gulls wheeled above the beach. The sun shone. In her hair, Mary wore the red ribbon her mother had given her. In her pinafore pocket was a scrap of soft upholsterer's velvet—Joseph's gift. Mary should have been happy, but she was sad. She had no gift from her father. Had he forgotten her tenth birthday?

She heard footsteps behind her.

"Happy birthday, daughter," her father said as he sat down beside her. He held one hand behind his back. "Close your eyes and hold out your hands."

Mary closed her eyes tightly and did as she was told.

"Now!" said Mr. Anning.

Mary opened her eyes. In her hands was a small chest of polished wood. It had a lid which could be lifted, and a tiny lock.

"A treasure chest for your favorite curiosities," said her father.

"Oh, father, it's beautiful," Mary cried. "I shall keep it forever!" She set the chest down and threw her arms around her father. "Thank you."

Mr. Anning rose from the steps. "Have a good birthday, little daughter. Let me know when the stagecoach arrives."

After he went into the house, Mary sat for awhile with the beautiful treasure chest in her lap. "Later, I will line it with the velvet Joseph gave me," she said to herself.

Mary jumped up. She hurried to her room and carefully put the chest in the back of the clothes press. It would be safe there. She picked up her skipping rope and ran back outside. What a wonderful birthday! Mary was so happy she felt she would explode. She started to skip.

"Higgledy, piggledy, my black hen . . .", she began to chant. But before she could say, "She lays eggs for gentlemen . . ." the wheels of the stagecoach could be heard on the road above Lyme Regis. Mary dropped the rope.

"Father," she called. It's the stagecoach!"

Mr. Anning came to the door. "We're ready for them," he said with a smile.

The curiosities which Mary and her father had collected were now washed, polished, and arranged for the summer visitors.

Suddenly, with a great clatter, the stagecoach plunged down the steep, rough road into Lyme Regis. It raced down the street, and stopped in a cloud of dust, at the inn.

The ladies who stepped from the stagecoach wore lovely large bonnets, and dresses with flowing skirts of soft, colorful materials. The men were dressed in handsome coats and skin-tight trousers. On their heads were tall black beaver top hats.

One of the ladies wore an enormous pink bonnet.

"How can she hold her head up?" Mary asked her father.

The minute she stepped out of the coach, Pink Bonnet began to talk.

"Oh, this lovely air," she cried. "What a joy to smell the sea again. I can still feel the wretched smoke of London in my nose!"

Blue Bonnet followed her from the coach.

"I *love* the sea," she cried.

One of the gentlemen passengers laughed. "Then the writer, Mr. Horace Walpole, was correct," he said.

"How is that?" asked Pink Bonnet.

"He once wrote, 'One would think that the English were ducks; they are forever waddling to the waters.' "

"How quaint," said Blue Bonnet.

Mary giggled. She could just see them—English gentlemen in top hats, and ladies in huge bonnets—quacking happily as they waddled eagerly down to Lyme Bay.

After the coach was emptied of its passengers, hat boxes, satchels, and valises, it was driven into the stable yard of the inn. There the tired horses were fed and watered.

The passengers crowded into the inn, or drove away to their summer homes. After they were settled, many of them stopped at the Anning cottage to buy curiosities.

Petrified mollusks were their favorites. They took up very little room in the stuffed luggage of the visitors. After the summer was over, and the travelers had returned to their winter homes, these interesting curiosities would be placed on "what not" or "curio" shelves to be admired by those who had not been to Lyme Regis.

One evening, while Mrs. Anning was visiting a sick friend, Mary prepared her father's tea. As she poured it, she said, "Father, do you think the people who buy our curiosities will remember where they bought them after they return home?"

"Perhaps not, lass," her father replied.

"Then I will make them remember. I shall paint *In Memory of Lyme Regis* on every shell."

"You will find it hard to paint such a message on the horns of ammon and the thunderstones."

"Then I shall paint the clam shells. Perhaps they'll sell better."

Mr. Anning smiled at Mary. "We will have to charge a few more farthings."

"People like things that are different," said Mary. "They'll be glad to pay more."

And, sure enough, every day more and more farthings, pence, and shillings filled the money box. Mary soon learned to bargain with customers. She became known as a shrewd trader.

Mary was so busy helping her father that she had little time to play "follow-the-leader" up and down the Cobb.

"Mary, Mary, quite contrary, how do your 'curios' grow?" the children yelled.

Mary paid no attention. She thought them quite silly to be playing such a dangerous game. They were always falling off the Cobb and getting horrid bumps on their heads.

But when the summer visitors went "dipping" in the bay, Mary took a few minutes off from her work to watch the fun with the rest of the children.

Most of the visitors did not dress on the beach and wade into the water as the children did. They were carried there in curious, square, big-wheeled carriages called "bathing machines." The bathing machines were drawn into the water by horses. Then the bathers were dipped up and down quickly in the salty water by two strong men or women.

"They wear so many clothes," Mary said to herself. "It's a wonder they ever feel the water."

When the bathers had dipped long enough, they were helped back into the bathing machine. Then the machine with its dripping passengers was pulled back to dry land, followed by shouting and laughing boys who splashed water on the carriage and horses.

Mary could not understand why anyone would want to bathe in this curious way. She loved the feel of the water on her bare feet. The thought of jumping into the bay with most of her clothes on was not at all pleasant.

It was fun to watch the summer visitors. But most of all, Mary enjoyed the company of her father. She loved to trudge along behind him as he strode down the beach and across the meadow which lay between Lyme Regis and Charmouth, two miles to the east.

One day, as they neared Charmouth, they met a boy Mary had not seen before. He was picking up shells.

"Good day," he said. "Are you collecting, too?"

"We are," said Mr. Anning. "What is your name, lad?"

"I am Henry De la Beche," the boy replied. "My mother and I live in Charmouth. My father was a naval officer. He died when I was very young. I am home on a holiday from the military academy at Great Harlow."

"Are you going to be an officer?" asked Mary.

"Perhaps," said Henry.

Mary liked Henry. He wasn't as silly as the other boys. He was the same age as Joseph, so Mary felt quite at ease with him. After the first meeting, they often went curiosity hunting together. Joseph joined them when he could get away from the upholstery shop.

One evening, a little black and white dog followed Mary home. No one came to claim him, so he became Mary's dog. She called him Tray.

Tray loved to go curiosity hunting. He was wonderful company for Mary, especially when no one else could go with her.

Mr. Anning frequently stayed home. He still had a bad cough and was quite thin. Mary worried about him.

Then one terrible day, Mr. Anning collapsed and died quite suddenly. Mrs. Anning was so grief-stricken she paid little attention to her children. For the first time in her life, Mary felt very

much alone. She kept listening for her father's footsteps, but of course he didn't come.

For a while Mary did very little curiosity hunting. She would walk slowly down the steps which led to the beach, or climb to the highest part of the Cobb. There she would sit with Tray nestled in her arms, and look out at the sea. The children called to her, "Mary Ann, Mary Ann, come play 'puss-in-the-corner' with us."

But Mary shook her head.

Henry climbed up on the Cobb beside her. "I'm sorry," he said.

Mary squeezed back the tears.

"I'll be all right," she replied.

CHAPTER FOUR

Mary's Monster

One day Mary woke early and jumped out of bed. "I'm going back to work," she said aloud. "Father would not want me to mope about."

She slipped on her pattens, tied her bonnet securely under her chin, and picked up her basket, hammer, and chisel. Then she set out for the cliffs with Tray scampering ahead of her.

Mary worked all day. When evening came, she felt much better.

After a time, Mary became used to working without her father. Slowly her store of curiosities grew larger and more in-

teresting. Among them was a strange skull over two feet long. It had a long mouth full of sharp teeth. Joseph found it, quite by accident, and gave it to her.

"I think the rest of it is somewhere in the cliff near Charmouth," he said.

Mary thought the skull was that of a crocodile. She put it away on a shelf with some other strange bones she had found.

Mary became better acquainted with the Philpot sisters who lived on Silver Street not far from the Anning cottage. They had been customers of Mary's father. Both of them were fascinated with curiosities. They bought a great many from Mary, and encouraged her to carry on her father's work.

The extra money helped the family a great deal since Joseph was paid very little as an apprentice in the upholstery shop.

One night after Mary went to bed, the wind blew and blew. It rained hard. The waters of the bay crashed high on the beach and even splashed over the highest part of the Cobb. As Mary listened to the wild storm, she said to herself, "Tomorrow morning, I'll go to the cliffs near Charmouth. The storm will have washed away earth and stone from them. Perhaps I can collect some bigger curiosities which will fetch me a better price."

The next morning, Mary got up early and set out for the cliffs.

It was a beautiful day in the year 1811. Mary was almost twelve years old. The sun shone as if there had been no storm. But the beach was littered with debris and overturned fishing boats. Tray ran this way and that, sniffing at the strange new objects the storm had left behind.

"Come along, Tray," said Mary. "We have work to do."

This morning, Mary noticed that the cliffs had lost great chunks of soil and rock which now lay in piles at their base. Very carefully she began to search for curiosities, keeping an eye out for falling rock.

As Mary peered at the cliffs, something unusual caught her eye. She saw what seemed to be bones lying in the rock in front of her.

She tapped the crumbling rock with her hammer. Chunks of it fell away. Mary tapped again. More bones appeared. She backed away for a better look. "What *is* it?" she thought.

With her chisel, Mary carefully lifted away pieces of the splintered rock. Underneath lay other bones. Finally, a huge backbone with large curving ribs attached, stood out as the rock continued to fall away.

Tray was beside himself at the sight of so many bones. He barked frantically and ran back and forth in front of the cliff.

Mary's heart pounded with excitement. What had she found?

She walked along the cliff face a few feet, tapping as she went. At every tap, more bones appeared, until the skeleton of a strange, unknown animal began to take shape. Even though its head was missing, Mary was quite sure this creature was no crocodile.

"It's a *monster*," Mary cried, "A monster curiosity—trapped in the rock exactly like the smaller curiosities! But what can it be? Where is its head?" Then Mary remembered. The skull that Joseph gave her—could that be it? She would find out as soon as she could remove this huge curiosity from the cliff.

Curiosities must be handled with care. Mary knew that. But how in the world did a person handle a curiosity as big as this one?

As Mary stood there wondering how she could get the monster safely out of the cliff, Henry ran down the beach toward her.

"What is *that*?" he yelled.

"I don't know."

"What are you going to do with it?"

Mary thought a bit. "I'll hire the quarrymen," she said. "They can cut it out of the cliff for me."

"I'll fetch them," Henry cried as he darted away.

"Wait," said Mary. "Tell Joseph to bring the head."

"The head! What head?"

"Just tell him to bring it. He'll know."

While Henry was gone, Mary took her hammer and chisel and began to peck out an outline around the skeleton. Now the quarrymen would know where to cut.

It was almost an hour before Henry and Joseph came running back with the quarrymen lumbering after them. Joseph carried the "crocodile" skull in his arms. As soon as he saw the bones in the cliff he shouted, "You found it, Mary. You found the rest of it!" He ran to the skeleton and held the skull at the end where the head should have been.

What a fearsome thing the creature became when the ugly head was added. Now it was a monster twice as long as Joseph was tall. It had short flippers or feet. Its sharp teeth looked ready to bite. And its enormous eye socket seemed to glare at those who stared at it.

The quarrymen stopped in astonishment when they saw the strange skeleton with its monstrous head.

"Lor' ha' mercy," one of them yelled. "What heathen creature is that?"

"I won't go near it," shouted another. "It's the work of the devil!"

The third quarryman laughed. "It's only bones," he cried. "Bones can't hurt you!"

"He's right," said Mary. "Now will you please cut the skeleton out of the cliff for me?"

The quarrymen put their heads together and discussed the matter. After much argument they agreed to help Mary.

"How much will you pay?" they asked.

Mary did not want to part with any of her small savings. But the only way she could get the monster out of the cliff was with the help of the quarrymen. "Whatever you say," she said.

So the quarrymen decided on a small sum which pleased even Mary, and set to work with their hammers, saws, and chisels.

It took most of the afternoon for the quarrymen, with the help of Joseph and Henry, to remove the monster from its resting place. Tray stood guard, and Mary gave directions as the skeleton was carefully cut into pieces small enough to lift.

Mary had not eaten since morning. So between directions, she shared with Tray bits of bread and cheese from her pinafore pocket. But her mind was so full of ideas as to what the monster might be, she scarcely knew she had eaten.

"What *can* it be?" she said to herself. "Is it a fat crocodile, or a thin whale? Or is it something different—something from one of those other worlds father told me about?"

By the time the skeleton was removed from the cliff, people had gathered from everywhere to see what was going on.

"What *is* it? What *can* it be?" they cried as they crowded closer. "Is it a crocodile? Is it a *dragon*?"

Henry pushed them aside. "I'll go fetch Dr. Everard Home," he said. "He is the king's physician and is visiting in Lyme Regis.

He knows a great deal about human bones. Perhaps he can tell us what Mary's creature is."

"I'll go, too," Joseph called. "I have to get back to work."

In the meantime, Mr. Henley, the lord of the manor, came

puffing up. He bought curiosities to sell to museums. When he saw Mary's monster he said, "I'll buy it!"

Mary would rather have kept her monster. It was the biggest curiosity she had ever seen. But where could she put it? No shelf in her house would hold such a large skeleton.

"How much?" asked Mary.

"Twenty-three pounds," Mr. Henley replied.

Twenty-three pounds was a great many farthings. It sounded like a fortune to Mary.

"Sold," she said.

Just then Henry arrived with Dr. Home in tow.

"I met him on the way," he shouted. "He was coming to see what was going on."

Dr. Home hurried up to the skeleton. He examined it carefully from head to tail.

"Is it a crocodile?" Mary asked.

"No," Dr. Home replied. "But it may be another type of reptile, or perhaps a member of the whale family. Whatever it is, it's the first of its kind I have ever seen. This is a great discovery you have made, lass."

Mary sighed. "Would *anyone* know what it is?"

"I will consult with other scientists at once," said Dr. Home. "Together we should come up with an answer. But in the meantime, for want of a better name, we'll simply have to call the skeleton "The Mystery of Lyme Regis.""

CHAPTER FIVE

Monsters and More Monsters

As soon as scientists heard of Mary's fantastic discovery, they flocked to Lyme Regis. Some had seen petrified bones of such a creature before, but not assembled in an almost perfect skeleton. Museums were so eager to locate other specimens, they paid good prices for any bones brought to them. Soon everyone was hunting for monsters.

It was a strange sight to see ladies in flowing skirts and big bonnets scrambling about the cliffs carrying fossil hammers and frilly parasols.

But the strangest sight was that of the gentlemen who

searched for bones while wearing their tall black beaver *top hats*.

Quarrymen, butchers, bakers, children—anyone who wanted to earn extra money—set out for the cliffs with their hammers and baskets. They were no longer afraid of strange skeletons. They began to call curiosities "fossils" just as the scientists did.

One of the scientists who came to Lyme Regis was William Buckland of Oxford University. Mary liked him at once. He had such a jolly twinkle in his eye.

"Miss Anning," he said. "Would you care to show me where you found your mysterious creature?"

Mary was delighted to have such an important person interested in her discovery. So the two of them, with Tray in the lead, went tramping off to the Charmouth cliffs where the monster had lain; Mary with her basket, and William Buckland with his big blue fossil bag and tall top hat.

As they neared the cliffs Tray raced ahead with excited yelps. He stopped suddenly at a pile of rocks.

"That's the place," said Mary. "Tray remembers it. I found the skeleton there—in the blue Lias layer of the cliff."

Mary and her scientist friends could tell that the earth was in layers, or strata. But not even William Smith, nicknamed "Strata Smith" because of his great knowledge of the strata of England, knew that the Lias was the oldest layer, or stratum of the Jurassic period of earth. This period, un-named in Mary's time, began

about 180,000,000 years ago. It was an age when great dinosaurs roamed the earth, and flying reptiles and bird-like creatures began to appear.

Other strange bones found in England had not yet been identified as dinosaur bones. Many uneducated people still thought they were the remains of dragons, elephants, or of giants. So Mary and her friends had no way of knowing that the "Mystery of Lyme Regis" had lived at the same time the giant Brontosaurus, the weird-looking Stegosaurus, and the fierce Allosauras were tromping about the earth.

After William Buckland returned to Oxford, Mary went on about her business. Her steady customers were still Margaret and Elizabeth Philpot, H. H. Henley, and a Colonel Birch who frequently visited Lyme Regis.

When Mary was fourteen years old she found a new friend, a Mrs. Stock, who gave Mary her first geology book. This book was a great help. Now Mary could study the strata with greater knowledge. She learned to call horns of ammon "ammonities," and thunderstones "belemnites." She began to recognize other forms of fossils such as footprints in rocks.

Once, at a party, Mary's jolly friend, William Buckland, showed the guests how fossil footprints were made, by imitating a hen waddling through mud. It was such a funny sight everyone howled with laughter. But no one ever forgot this lesson on fossil footprints.

Seven years passed and Mary's monster still had no name.

Finally, in 1818, George Koenig, of the British Museum said, "Everyone agrees the creature is a sea-going reptile with a fish-like shape, so why not call it Ichthyosaurus after the Greek words *Ichthyo* meaning 'fish,' and *sauros* meaning 'lizard.' "

George Cuvier of France, and the English scientists, Dr. Charles Lyell, Richard Owen, and William Buckland agreed with him.

But Dr. Home would have none of it. He called Mary's monster Proteosaurus after a cave salamander named Proteus.

Then in 1820, another scientist, Rev. William Conybeare, declared that Ichthyosaurus was a better name. His friend, Henry De la Beche, who had given up a military career to become a geologist, agreed. "I commend it," he said.

And that was that—Ichthyosaurus, fish-lizard. It must have been a good name for it hasn't changed to this day.

In 1821, Mary discovered another monster. It, too, was a sea reptile. It had a short wide body with four large paddles, and a long, long neck.

"It looks like a turtle shell with a snake threaded through it," said the merry William Buckland.

When William Conybeare and Henry De la Beche saw this creature, they called it Plesiosaurus—nearly like a lizard.

Three years later, in 1824, Mary found another Plesiosaurus with an unusually long neck. She sold this one to the Duke of

Buckingham for one hundred pounds. At this time, she also uncovered the skeletons of two large Ichthyosauri.

During the next few years so many Ichthyosauri were found that this creature became known as Ichthyosaurus Communis—common fish-lizard. Some of them were nearly thirty feet long.

Mary now lived in a shop fronted cottage on Broad Street. She and her mother had moved there in 1826.

Two years later, Mary discovered the skeleton of a very different creature. It was a flying reptile—the remote ancestor of the first bird. Because of the long finger which edged the wing, it was called Pterodactyl—wing finger.

All these discoveries had a great effect on the scientists of the time. One of them was Charles Darwin, who later developed a theory about the evolution of living things.

Mary's fame spread. On June 27, 1832, Dr. Gideon Mantell, who discovered the first dinosaur bones, came to see Mary Anning. In his journal written later, he said, ". . . We sallied out in quest of Mary Anning, the geological *lioness* of the place . . .".

Mary kept on hunting for monsters. Her startling discoveries sparked a monster hunt which was to spread all over the world and extend into the present time. The creatures she discovered were remarkable. But so was Mary. For no other woman of her day made the study and selling of fossils her full-time profession. Most young women were content to be housewives or governesses. In a few cases, they were writers like Jane Austen, who lived for a time in a rambling white cottage on Lyme bay; or Ann Radcliffe, whose fascinating horror stories were carried away from circulating libraries by the armful.

Anna Maria Pinney and Lucy Oakes, Mary's friends, sometimes accompanied her on her fossil hunts, but found it dangerous work, for Mary climbed cliffs and dared high tides without fear.

Scientists and other important people continued to come to Mary's shop. One day the king of Saxony dropped in and bought a baby Ichthyosaurus, six feet long. He paid fifteen pounds for it.

Mary enjoyed her friendships with these people—"big wigs," as she called them. But she was kind to the needy, and patient

with the children who came to her shop to spend their pennies on tiny polished ammonites. She took care of her mother for the rest of her life.

As Mary grew older, she did not have to worry too much about money. At William Buckland's suggestion, the English government gave her enough pounds to last her until she died.

Many of Mary's monsters can now be seen at the British Museum of Natural History in London, where there is also a picture of Mary with her old dog Tray.

When Mary died, in 1847, she was truly famous—so much so that in the church on the edge of the cliffs at Lyme Regis, there is a stained glass window in memory of Mary Anning. Under it is a plaque which says:

> *This window is sacred to the memory of Mary Anning, of this parish, who died March 9, 1847, and is erected by the Vicar of Lyme, and some of the members of the Geological Society of London, in commemoration of her usefulness in furthering the science of geology, as also of her benevolence of heart, and integrity of life.*

On February 18, 1848, Sir Henry De la Beche paid a final tribute to his life-long friend. In his Presidential address to the

Geological Society of London, he praised Mary Anning for her valuable contribution to the science of geology.

The scientists who heard his words of praise, remembered Mary with affection and great pride. For all of them knew that, in 1811, Mary and her monster had helped open the door to the far-distant and fascinating past of all living things.

SOURCES

Austen, Jane, *Persuasion*, Harcourt Library of English and American Classics, New York, Harcourt, Brace and World, Inc., 1962. Description of Lyme Regis, pp. 94-96, 104.

Bailey, Edward, *Charles Lyell*, New York, Doubleday and Co., Inc., 1963. Mary's friendship with Buckland, p. 35. Hunt fossils in top hats, p. 35.

Colbert, Edwin H., *Dinosaurs—Their Discovery and Their World*, New York, E. P. Dutton and Co., 1961, pp. 143-144.

Epstein, Sam and Beryl, *Prehistoric Animals*, New York, Franklin Watts, Inc., 1956, pp. 5-8, 110-113.

Heath, Frank R. (Revised by E. T. Long), *Dorset, The Little Guides*, London, B. T. Batsford Ltd., 1949.

Kurten, Bjorn, *The Age of Dinosaurs*, New York, McGraw Hill Book Co., 1968, pp. 16, 23, 79, 111, 174-175.

Lang, W. D., "Mary Anning of Lyme, Collector and Vendor of Fossils 1799-1847," *Natural History Magazine* (British), Vol. 5, 1935, pp. 64-81.

——"Mary Anning (1799–1847) and Other Pioneer Geologists of Lyme," *Proceedings Dorset Natural History and Archeological Society*, Vol. 60, 1939, pp. 142-164.

——"Three Letters of Mary Anning, Fossilist of Lyme," *Proceedings Dorset Natural History Society*, Vol. 66, 1945, pp. 169-173. Mary comments on risks of fossil hunting, p. 170. Dates of various discoveries, p. 172.

——"More About Mary Anning, Including a Newly Found Letter," *Proceedings Dorset Natural History Society*, Vol. 71, 1950, pp. 184-188. Mary credits father for her knowledge of fossils, p. 186. Children buy fossils, p. 187. Mary's dog, Tray, p. 188.

——"Mary Anning and the Fire at Lyme," *Proceedings Dorset Natural History Society*, Vol. 74, 1953, pp. 175-177. A good description of the streets of Lyme Regis, p. 176.

____"Mary Anning and Anna Maria Pinney," *Proceedings Dorset Natural History Society*, Vol. 76, 1956, pp. 146-152. King of Saxony's visit, p. 150. Mary's "big wigs," p. 150. Mantell's quote about Mary's fame, and the rough road to Lyme Regis, p. 151.

____"Mary Anning's Escape From Lighting," *Proceedings Dorset Natural History Society*, Vol. 80, 1959, pp. 91-93. Her brother Joseph's part in the discovery, p. 92.

____"Portraits of Mary Anning and Other Items," *Proceedings Dorset Natural History Society*, Vol. 81, 1960, pp. 89-91. The naming of Mary's monster, p. 89.

Ludovici, L. J., *The Great Tree of Life—Paleontology: The Natural History of Living Creatures*, New York, G. P. Putnam Sons, 1963. Early theories about fossils, pp. 16, 17.

Lyme Regis, Official Guide, Issued by the Borough Publicity Association, Lyme Regis, England, 1974.

Opie, Iona and Peter, *Children's Games in Street and Playground*, Oxford, Clarendon Press, 1969.

"*Proceedings at the Annual General Meeting, 18th February, 1848*," *Journal of the Geographical Survey of London*, Vol. 4, London, Longman, Brown, Green, and Longmans, 1848. Tribute to Mary Anning by Henry De la Beche in his presidential address at the Geological Society meeting.

Rhodes, Frank H. T., Zim, Herbert S., Shaffer, Paul R., *Fossils, A Guide To Prehistoric Life*, New York, Golden Press, 1962. According to these writers the Jurassic age began 180,000,000 years ago, p. 52. Length of Ichthyosauri, up to thirty feet, p. 143.

Wendt, Herbert, *Before the Deluge*, New York, Doubleday and Co., Inc., 1968, pp. 8-10, 19, 110-113.

White, R. J., *Life in Regency England*, London, Batsford Ltd., 1963. Horace Walpole quote ". . . the English were ducks . . .", p. 131. Bathing machines, p. 129. Horror stories, pp. 153-155.

Woodward, H. B., Ussher, W. A. E., *Memoirs of the Geological Survey—England and Wales—The Geology of the Country Near Sidmouth and Lyme Regis*, Second Edition, London, Darling and Son Ltd., 1911. Curiosities (fossils) sold to passengers on coaches, Introduction. H. H. Henley, lord of the manor at Lyme Regis, p. 33. Length of some Ichthyosauri found there, 28 feet, p. 33.

Yarwood, Doreen, *Outline of English Costume*, Boston, Publisher's Plays Inc., 1967.

A NOTE FROM THE AUTHOR

All the characters named in this story are real people. I am grateful to these folk of the past for their contribution to this book.

I also wish to give my heartfelt thanks to certain people of the present—

To my husband, Glenn M. Blair, for giving me the benefit of his writing expertise in the many careful and patient readings of *Mary's Monster*, and for his encouragement—

To my daughter-in-law, Mim, and my son, Glenn M. Blair Jr., for their research on my behalf in London—

To my daughter, Sally Leach, for her careful editing of some of my earlier writing efforts—

To Barbara Lalicki of Coward, McCann & Geoghegan, for her excellent suggestions—

To A. P. Harvey, Librarian, British Museum (Natural History), London, and to H. Chessell, Hon. Curator, the Philpot Museum, Lyme Regis, for his assistance in sources—

And to Mary Jane Snyder, my good friend, for the loan of books, a listening ear, and the suggestion that I write a child's story about Mary Ann Anning.

R. V. B.